Teaching the Bible
with Puppets

Including
Instructions for Making
Puppets and Sets

Teaching the Bible WITH Puppets

JEANNE S. FOGLE

XXIII
TWENTY-THIRD PUBLICATIONS
Mystic, Connecticut

Twenty-Third Publications
185 Willow Street
P.O. Box 180
Mystic, CT 06355
(203) 536-2611

ISBN 0-89622-405-8
Library of Congress Catalog Number 89-50563

Contents

Introduction

Puppet Plays

Teaching the Bible
with Puppets

Introduction

Many teachers feel intimidated by the idea of using drama in religious education and Bible School sessions. Some might believe that puppet dramas are beyond their skills or just too much trouble. The fact is that there is no easier way to teach biblical truths and understandings than by having children act out the stories. We know that children learn by doing. Role playing comes naturally to them; it is what children do instinctively. Pretending is one of the earliest play experiences that we all have. So why not take advantage of this natural instinct by having children tell the story with all the joy and spontaneity that can happen when they are freed to express themselves creatively?

Storytelling is an important element of religious education and Bible School sessions, for the primary purpose is to share and teach the word. Children today live in a world where communication is designed to be a totally sensory experience. The commercials they see and hear, the television programs they are teased into viewing, the activities they are enticed to try—even the very way they are encouraged to act and react are all dramatically presented with auditory and visual messages that fill their senses. Telling the Bible story in the same way week after week is not likely to hold the interest of today's child. Allowing the child to dramatize the story involves using emotions and experiences, and, when that happens, both the listeners and the participants become more involved.

Puppet shows and plays need not be elaborate to be meaningful and entertaining. It is simply not practical to present elaborate productions within the weekly session. In fact, creative expression is often hampered when materials and projects are too complicated.

I prefer to have children create their own scripts and present their own interpretation of stories and situations. Before this can happen, however, both the teacher and the child need to feel comfortable using dramatic activities in their particular setting. As the scripts and ideas in this book are used and as dramatic activities are included more frequently in lessons, it is hoped that the teachers will become more comfortable with this type of activity and the children will be encouraged to interpret the stories in their own way. It will happen. All you need is more practice using puppets and role playing activities. The best part is that the storytelling part of the lesson will be more exciting for the whole class.

The scripts in this book have been written in an upbeat manner using contemporary dialogue and familiar situations. Children will relate more to basic biblical truths and understandings if they recognize even a small part of their world in the story.

Although these scripts have been written for puppets, they can easily be adapted for dramatic presentation with the children assuming the roles of the various characters in the story.

The scripts have been kept brief so that they may be used conveniently within the lesson period of the weekly church school session.

So get rid of your trepidation and fear of losing control of the class by allowing the children to present the message. Rethink and reevaluate the use of dramatic activities in your lessons. No one, least of all the children, expects a major theatrical production. Allowing the children to share in telling the wonderful story of our faith enriches their experience and makes the Scriptures more meaningful to them.

How and When to Use Puppets

In a weekly religious education class or church school session, puppets can be used to tell a story that reinforces the biblical truth or understanding contained in the lesson. Because it can be difficult to work with larger numbers of children, it is best to begin by using the puppet plays that call for fewer characters. Choose a story with two to six characters and select children to prepare the puppet play. Allow a helping teacher or an aide to work with the cast while other children are doing a separate activity. If you are the only adult with your group, you will need to recruit someone to help when you use puppet plays with your lesson. (Teenagers are excellent resource persons for this activity.)

The puppet play should be presented in the second half hour to allow puppeteers enough time to prepare and become familiar with the story they are to present. I really discourage the practice of preparing material one week to be used in the following week's session. The spontaneity is lost and expectations change when teachers and young participants have a week to fuss and fret over the "production."

I recommend having a set of simple puppets as part of the materials and resources for the church school class. On pages 9-10, there are patterns and suggestions for puppets that can be adapted to both biblical and contemporary settings. Providing a set of these puppets can be a great project for youth fellowship, women's organizations, or other church groups. We know of several churches that have had successful projects such as this.

There are occasions when children can make simple puppets to be used in the story. This can work very nicely when all of the children are involved in the presentation. When only a few children are involved, it becomes more practical to use the puppets on hand. Suggestions for making simple puppets may also be found on pages 8, 11-13.

The procedure for using puppets in Vacation Bible School is basically the same as for the weekly sessions. In this setting there are many other possibilities. Puppet plays prepared by classes or smaller groups may be shared with a larger audience in daily community or prayer time. The presentations may be used to reinforce the day's theme. Puppet plays could also be given at the closing service included in most Bible School schedules. The daily schedule allows more time for creative crafts that could include making all types of puppets.

Puppet dramas also work well with children's choirs. As a children's choir director, I am committed to helping choristers understand the meaning in the anthems they sing in worship. I often ask several children to come early to rehearsal in order to prepare a little play that may help to explain the music they are to perform.

Most important, please remember that these puppet shows and plays need not be confined to the classroom setting. Your own children can have a wonderful time with puppets and plays.

My own children spent many happy hours performing plays with other neighborhood children. These wonderful productions were presented in our backyard, our basement, and our living room to other friends and family— often to an audience of one or two. The joy and excitement of preparing and presenting those productions provided many happy memories for all of us.

Puppet Stage Construction

I approach this subject cautiously because, in most cases, the disadvantages of having permanent puppet stages outweigh the advantages. If these stages are built to last, they are usually too heavy and too cumbersome to move easily. If they are large enough for the children to work behind, they are probably too heavy and too large to store efficiently. Further, using these permanent stages helps to promote the (mistaken) idea that one needs an elaborate setting and much preparation in order to present puppet plays. For these reasons, I have chosen not to include plans for an enclosed permanent puppet stage.

A **makeshift puppet stage** that can be assembled quickly and easily will do nicely for regular church school sessions. Use an ordinary table with a cloth that reaches the floor or turn a table on its side to allow children to work behind it. Or place several chairs side by side facing away from the audience and cover them with a sheet or tablecloth.

One stage that impressed me was made with two wooden stands and a curtain hung on a closet rod. This stage was lightweight, easy to assemble, easy to store, and inexpensive to construct. The children had attached paper scenery to the front of the curtain. After the session the teacher rolled up the curtain and stored it and the two stands neatly in a closet. She recommended this stage because children can easily assemble it. *(See Figure 1.)*

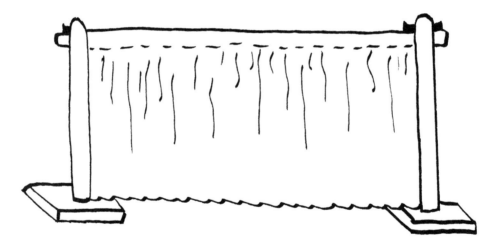

Figure 1

Here are the plans for this stage:

Materials
2 pieces of lumber - 2" x 2" x 4' (for stands)
2 pieces of lumber - 1" x 12" X 12" (for bases)
1 closet rod - 1" diameter
3 yards of 45" dark fabric
2 screw hooks

Procedure

1. Nail a 4' piece of lumber to base. Make a second stand.
2. Fasten hooks 1" from top of stand.
3. Fold longest side of fabric down 3 1/2". Sew a seam 3" from folded edge to make a casing for the strip.
4. Hem the fabric at the bottom edge so that curtain bottom reaches the floor.
5. Slip the rod through the casing.

If you plan to use puppets frequently in your church school program and if your church has ample facilities for presentation and storage, you may want to construct a **sturdier puppet stage**. *(See Figures 2 and 3 for front and rear views.)* It has worked well for us. It allows for several children to work behind the stage and it folds flat for easy storage.

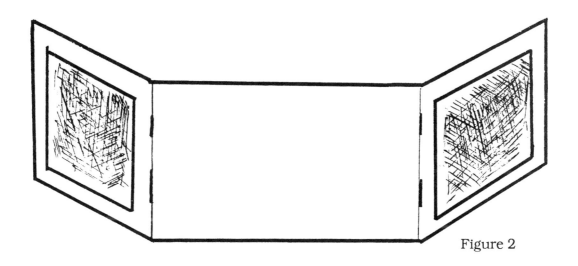

Figure 2

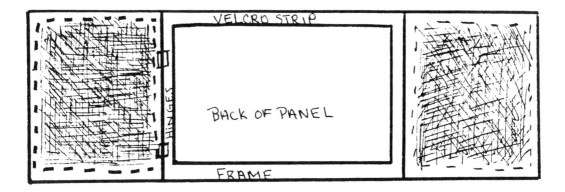

Figure 3

Materials
2 pieces of furring strip 1" x 2" x 6'
4 pieces of furring strip 1" x 2" x 4'
2 pieces of furring strip 1" x 2" x 2'
1 piece of masonite paneling 4' x 6'
2 pieces of burlap 2' x 4'
4 hinges
3 yards of velcro
balsa wood strips 1" wide, 3/16" thick cut in several lengths (3", 5", 7", 10")

Procedure
1. Make a frame that measures 4' x 6'.
2. Nail a 4' x 6' piece of masonite panel to the frame.
3. Make two smaller frames: 2' x 4'.
4. Cut burlap fabric to fit frame 2' x 4'. Staple burlap to frame. It is wise to glue edges to frame so burlap will not fray.
5. Lay large frame on floor—panel side down. Place two smaller frames on either side—burlap side up.
6. Attach two hinges to each corner.
7. We glued a velcro strip across the top of stage. We cut several lengths of balsa strips (3", 5", 7", 10") and glued a piece of velcro to bottom of strip. When we wanted to add a bit of scenery (houses, trees, etc.) above the stage, we just attached stick with velcro to the velcro strip on the frame. These sticks provided support for paper trees, houses, cars, animals, and other scenery that was taped to the strip. Other pieces of scenery may be taped to paneling in front of stage. A large manilla envelope glued to the back of the stage makes an ideal place to store support strips.

A **shadow puppet stage** is fairly easy to make. *(See Figure 4.)* For the screen, fasten a piece of white fabric to a large picture frame. To make the screen free-standing, mount it to two wooden supports that lie on the floor. *(See Figure 5 for a side view.)*

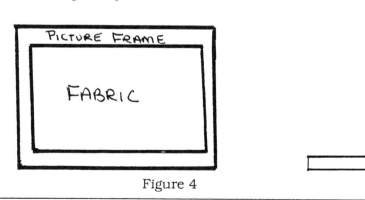

Figure 4   Figure 5

Be sure you have all equipment available and positioned properly for a shadow puppet presentation. *(See Figure 6.)*

Figure 6

Puppets Made for the Children

Basic story puppets are excellent to have on hand for children to use in the weekly religious education session or in daily Vacation Bible School. Having the puppets readily available allows for small groups of children to work independently on a puppet play presentation. Certainly, these puppets should be made to be more durable. We recommend making puppets of various age groupings and puppets that have different skin coloring. The addition of headdresses and robes can change contemporary characters into those that fit into a biblical setting.

Felt is recommended for the head of the puppet. Cut and sew on the seam line. Stuff with cotton batting or cloth pieces. Sew the bottom of the head shut but leave a small hole to insert finger. The eyes, nose, and ears may be made from felt and glued on. Mouth and eyebrows are embroidered onto the face. The hair is made from yarn sewn into the head. Special features like eyeglasses, freckles, or rosy cheeks may be added with all types of trims. The body of the puppet is made from fabric and decorated with buttons, ribbons, and trims. A robe pattern is included with the patterns because the children enjoy dressing the puppets and changing their appearance for different presentations. (*See Figures 7 and 8 on pages 9-10 for patterns.*)

Materials

Felt for head and felt pieces for features   Scissors
Fabric for body   Yarn
Trims   Yarn cotton batting

Sock puppets *(Figures 9 and 10)* are my favorite kind of puppets because they are fairly easy to make and they really can become characters of all types. Fill the top of an adult sock with cotton batting, cloth, or women's hosiery. Tie a ribbon or piece of yarn around the neck of the puppet. The

Figure 9

Figure 10

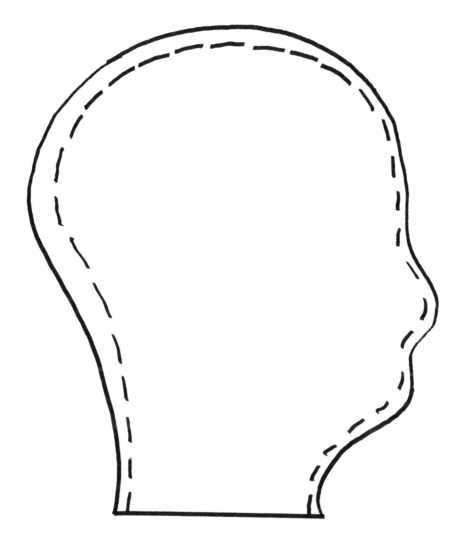

Figure 7

Figure 8

eyes, nose, and ears may be made with felt pieces. The mouth and eyebrows may be embroidered onto the face, or trim such as piping or rickrack will work nicely. Yarn attached to the head will make all types of hair styles. Felt hands may be attached to the sides of the sock. Buttons and trims are added to the body. Pieces of fabric should be hemmed and kept available to be used for biblical headdresses and robes.

Materials

Sock
Cotton Batting or Stuffing
Trims for features
Glue

Scissors
Felt Pieces
Fabric Squares

Stick puppets *(Figures 11 and 12)* are made from posterboard or heavy paper. Begin by having the children decide which puppets are needed for the story and what their distinguishing characteristics should be. Children often tend to make the figures too small to be seen at a distance, so it is good to remind them to make puppet figures that average about 12" in length. Draw the figures on posterboard or heavy paper. Cut them out. Decorate figures with felt markers, crayons, or paints. Trims such as sequins, buttons, ribbons, ribbon, yarn, fabric or felt pieces, rickrack, or lace may be added. Puppet figures are then glued or taped to wooden dowels.

Materials

posterboard or heavy paper
markers, crayons, pencils
glue

tape 1/4" wooden dowels - 12" lengths
trims and trinkets
scissors

Figure 11

Figure 12

Paper plate puppets *(Figure 13)* are excellent for younger children to make. Staple two small paper plates together with the bottoms on the outside. Decorate with markers, pencils, crayons, trims of all kinds. Glue a wooden dowel between two plates at the bottom.

Materials
paper plates
glue or stapler
tape
markers, crayons, pencils
trims and trinkets
fabric scraps
1/4" wooden dowel or popsicle sticks
scissors

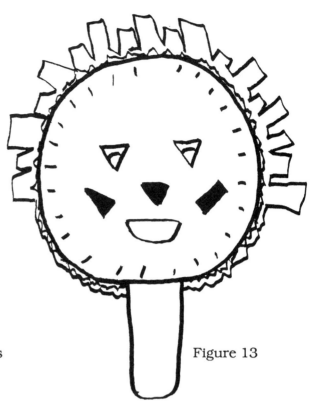

Figure 13

Figure 14

Paper bag puppets *(Figure 14)* are another good choice for younger children. The bottom of the bag becomes the face of the puppet. Children can draw features onto the bag with felt markers or crayons. Felt or fabric scraps, yarn, trims of all kinds, and buttons may be used to decorate the puppet.

Materials
paper bags - lunch size
felt markers, crayons
trims of all kinds
glue
felt or fabric scraps
scissors

Shadow puppets *(Figure 15)* are made in the same way as stick puppets except that black or dark posterboard is recommended to make the best silhouette. Shadow puppets are mounted on wooden dowels. The puppeteers stand behind a transparent screen. A bright light is projected onto the screen. The audience sees the silhouettes that tell the story. Remind the children to

concentrate on making some distinguishing characteristics for their shadow puppet so that the character will be easily recognized in the silhouette form.

Materials
dark posterboard
scissors
pencils
wooden dowels - 1/4"
glue or tape

Figure 15

One-piece **mitten puppets** are made from felt or stiffer fabric. We recommend having the puppet body cut and sewn together before the session. The children then add the features to the puppets. Felt pieces, fabric scraps, yarn, trims, buttons, and sequins may be added. The mitten shape design allows the children greater flexibility in moving the puppets. The procedure is to trace and cut out the puppet. Sew on seam line. Stuff head lightly with cotton batting or women's hosiery. Sew a seam at neckline but leave a hole for finger to fit through in order to move head. Add features and clothes if desired. *(See Figure 17 on page 14 for pattern.)*

Figure 16

Musical Accompaniment

Using "mood music" to begin and end puppet plays can really help everyone get into the spirit of the drama. All you need are tapes and a tape recorder. My list of recommended music includes:

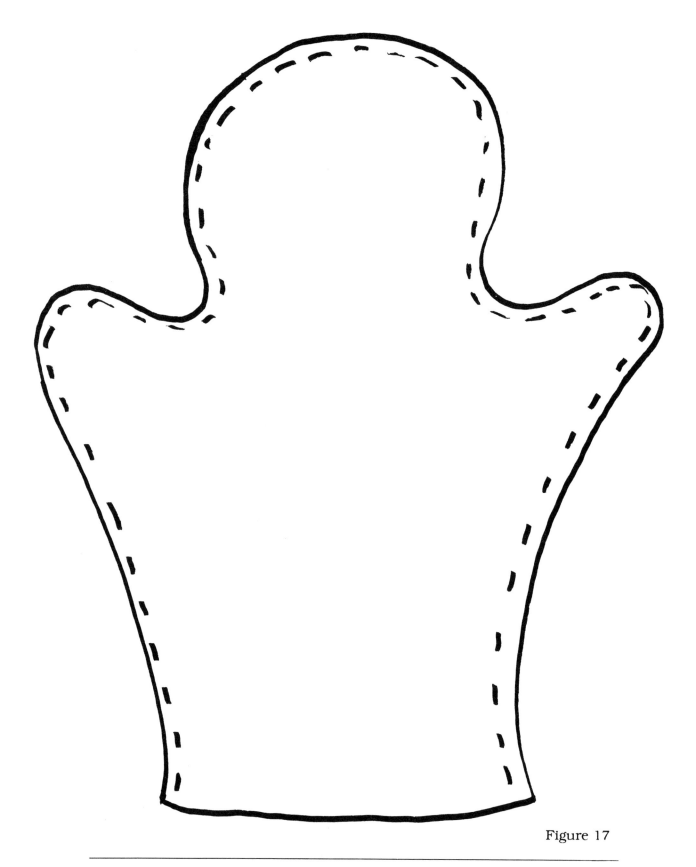

Figure 17

14

1. Classical music of all types, such as "Carmen," "Nutcracker Suite," "Swan Lake," "Hungarian Rhapsody," "Rhapsody in Blue," "1812 Overture," "Peer Gynt Suite," and any other selections that are dramatic in nature.
2. Overtures to operas or musicals
3. Spirituals
4. Folk music
5. Particular instrumental music— flute, brass, piano, bluegrass banjo
6. Film scores, such as "Star Wars," "2001: A Space Odyssey," or similar types.

Puppet Stage Backdrops

While a backdrop providing background scenery helps to enhance the story, it is not essential for puppet show presentations. Enclosed puppet stages usually have an area at the rear of the stage for a backdrop to be attached. Other stage arrangements would need to be set up so that a backdrop could be fastened to a wall or a screen behind the puppet action area.

Backdrops may be made from posterboard or cardboard and decorated with felt markers or crayons. Pellon with scenes painted with acrylic make a lovely backdrop, but it is time consuming and more expensive to make.

If time is limited in the sessions in which puppets are to be used, we suggest backdrops be made prior to these sessions.

When the puppet play is a total class project, children should be encouraged to make their own backdrops. Suggestions are given with each of the scripts in this book, but children may wish to create their own backdrop after they have read the story. *(See the illustrated suggestions on pages 16-17.)*

Background scenes should be very simple. Only a few colors should be used. Objects should be few in number and large enough to be visible. A cluttered backdrop is visually distracting and time consuming to make. Much more effective in puppet show presentations is the use of simple props or signs to help tell the story.

Babble at the Tower of Babel

Trading Places: Jacob and Esau

Gideon and the Midianites

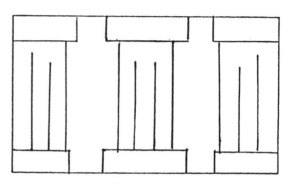

Joseph Forgives

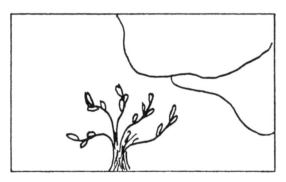

Moses and the Burning Bush

Solomon's Decision

Elijah's Contest with the Priests of Baal

The Story of Job

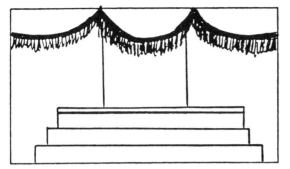

Queen Esther's Secret

Daniel and the Big Cats

The Miracle of the Loaves and Fishes

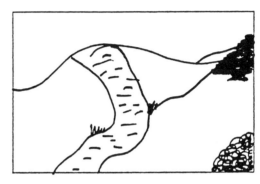

On the Road to Damascus

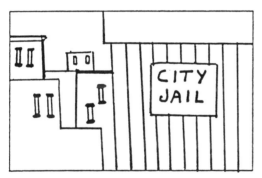

Paul, Silas, and the Earthquake

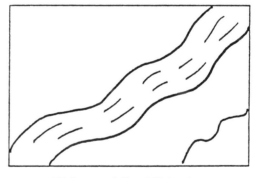

Philip and the Ethiopian

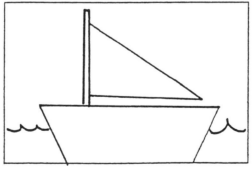

Paul and the Shipwreck

Babble at the Tower of Babel
(Based on the story in Genesis 11)

Characters: Narrator
Builder 1
Builder 2
King
Worker 1
Worker 2
Other workers

Props: Blocks

Background scenery: Building Site
Palace
At the tower

Scene One: At the building site

Builder 1   I tell you, this is unbelievable.

Builder 2   What?

Builder 1   That we can build a wall this strong, this high, and this fast.

Builder 2   You're right about that. Whoever invented this new mortar mix certainly was smart.

Builder 1   It works all right!

Builder 2   It sure does. If we keep going, this wall will be higher than the bushes, higher than the trees, higher than those mountains .

Builder 1   *(deep in thought)* Yeah.

Builder 2   Higher than the clouds, even!

Builder 1   That's a great idea. We should build a tower up to heaven.

Builder 2   Hey, I was just kidding.

Builder 1   Not me, friend. Let's discuss our plan with the king.

Builder 2   *(as they both leave the stage)* I was just kidding.

Scene Two: At the palace

King   Yes, gentlemen? I am told you wish to discuss some new building project with me— a new shopping center, perhaps, or maybe an extra special design for a new palace for me and the queen.

Builder 1	No, Your Majesty. We want to discuss building a tower.
King	A tower? We are already building one of those and I am told that from the top of it one can see the enemy coming two miles away.
Builder 1	Our tower will do that and more. We want to build a tower that is higher than any tower ever built.
King	That high, huh?
Builder 1	Yes, Your Majesty. So high that it will reach heaven.
King	Are you mad? Surely you joke!
Builder 2	He is not joking, Your Majesty.
Builder 1	No, Your Majesty, and when we get up to heaven, our enemies will be afraid because once we get up there, we will be as important and as powerful as God.
King	*(thoughtfully pacing back and forth)* Hmmm. Hmmm. You really think you can build this thing?
Builder 1	I know we can, Your Majesty, and now with this new mortar mix, the tower will be stronger than ever.
King	Well, all right. That *will* make us very important and very powerful. I shall tell my advisers to get the building materials for you and, of course, you will need help. All other building projects should stop, all play should stop, all meals and sleep time should be kept very short. We must make this our number one, most important project. Let's get busy. Think of it! Up to the sky!
Builder 2	*(as all three leave)* I was just kidding.
Narrator	The tower grew very fast because everyone was forced to work on it. The builders were excited about how high the tower was becoming. They could hardly wait until the tower was finished so that everyone would be forced to bow down to the mighty people of Babylon.
	Now the Lord God saw all of this and was very unhappy about the building project. God said, "These people are very foolish because this tower is only going to make the world more miserable. They want to sit in the top of the tower and play God. I must put a stop to this. I have a plan."

Scene Three: At the tower

King   Keep moving, builders. No time to soptick.

Builder 1   *(puzzled)* No time to soptick, pipnut?

King   *(angrily)* Pipnut! You called me a pipnut?

Builder 2   *(nervously)* Soptick, no, Huckleberry. Oh, pipnut. I was just icklebean.

Worker 1   We need a noodlenose over here to hold this sissypan in place.

King   *(even angrier)* You called me a noodlenose?

Worker 2   And we need the billybong to make this picklepuss stick.

King   *(angrier than ever)* You called me a picklepuss!

Worker 1   *(upset)* Sok mut pup tent!

Worker 2   *(confused)* Tut lik ong su!

Builder 1   *(very impatient)* Wot si bim too!

Builder 2   *(frightened)* Dipple doo dun lip!

King   *(throwing up his hands in despair)* Huckleberry! Pup tent! Oh, fudge!

Narrator   Soon, the people were all speaking in strange, new languages. They looked at one another in alarm and became very frightened about what was happening. Some of the people ran from Babylon and took their new languages to faraway places. And those who stayed behind? Well, they continued to work on the tower for awhile, but since they could not understand one another, the tower grew very slowly. In all the confusion, the people soon forgot what they were building and the unfinished tower was left standing in the middle of the town square. Visitors who later came there just thought the funny old tower was a modern art piece.

From that time on, there were different languages among all the people and nations of the earth.

Trading Places: Jacob and Esau
(Based on the story in Genesis 25)

Characters: Narrator   Props: Spoon for stirring soup
               Rebekah   Bowl for soup
               Jacob   Pieces of fur
               Esau   Extra clothes for Jacob
               Isaac   Vegetables for soup

Background Scene: Inside a tent

Narrator   Abraham's son Isaac married Rebekah and they settled in the land of Canaan. Many years later, they became the parents of twin sons. The first to be born was Esau, who had a red complexion and lots of hair. He was not likely to win any baby beauty contests. Then came Jacob who was pale and smooth skinned. He was a real charmer.

Esau was a regular outdoors guy. He liked to fish and to trap. In fact, he became a mighty hunter, which made his father happy since Esau helped to bring home the bacon. Esau was definitely number one in his father's book. Jacob, on the other hand, didn't care much for the rough and tough stuff and so he spent most of his time with his mother. He learned to cook and to clean, and to repair the tents. He became a whiz in political matters and he was the apple of his mother's eye.

Rebekah   Jacob, dear, I must go to an all-day meeting of my sewing circle. Will you take care of things for me while I am gone?

Jacob   Yes, mother.

Rebekah   Sweep the floor, shake the rugs, and make a pot of soup for dinner.

Jacob   Yes, mother. I think I will make my special lentil soup. Everyone loves my lentil soup.

Rebekah   Wonderful. We shall have dinner at six o'clock. Please have it ready then. *(She leaves the stage.)*

Jacob   *(as he prepares the soup)* Oh, I just love making soup. First the meat— stir, stir— then in go the delicious lentils— stir, stir— some juicy turnips— stir, stir— and some freshly baked rutabagas— stir, stir. *(singing)* Umm, umm, good; Umm, umm, good; That's what Jacob's soups are, Umm, umm, good.

Esau *(enters)* Oh, I'm about to die. I'm starving. Give me some soup.

Jacob I can't. Not now.

Esau Why not?

Jacob It is for dinner at six o'clock. I have my orders.

Esau But I'll die of starvation. I've been out hunting and I'm famished. I need food right now. I can't wait till six o'clock.

Jacob Sorry

Esau Please?

Jacob I can't.

Esau You can.

Jacob I can't.

Esau Please, I'll do anything.

Jacob *(thoughtfully)* Anything?

Esau Yes, anything. Name your price.

Jacob Will you give me your birthright and allow me to be the head of the family when father dies?

Esau Well, maybe not that!

Jacob Well, then it is dinner at six.

Esau What good is my birthright if I am dead from hunger? O.K., O.K., you win. Now give me some soup.

Jacob Coming right up.

Narrator So Jacob gave Esau all the soup he wanted. Esau forgot all about the bargain but Jacob did not forget. Now Isaac became very old and quite ill. Just before he died, Isaac called Esau to his bedside.

Isaac Esau? Is that you, son? I can't see a thing these days.

Esau   It's me, father.

Isaac   Take your bow and arrow, Esau, and hunt a wild deer on the plain. Cook it just the way I like it so I can have my favorite meal before I die. Then I will give you my blessing to be the head of this family.

Esau   I will do that, father. *(Esau leaves.)*

Rebekah   *(at the other side of the stage)* Uh, oh! Jacob, dear. We have a little problem here. Unless we act and act fast, Esau will be the new head of this family and that might not be such a good idea.

Jacob   I know. Esau traded me his birthright for my lentil soup and a deal is a deal, but father will never go for that.

Rebekah   Well, I have a little plan. Come and let me tell you. *(They leave the stage.)*

Narrator   And so, the clever Rebekah dressed Jacob in his brother's clothing, which really had a special smell—not good. And she covered Jacob's arms and head with the hairy skin of a goat—ugh! Next, she gave Jacob a bowl of wonderful stew, fit for a king, and sent him to his father's bedside.

Jacob   I'm back and here is your favorite meal, father.

Isaac   *(Eats from the bowl.)* Oh, thank you. It is delicious. Come nearer, my son.

Jacob   Here I am, father. Now, may I have your blessing?

Isaac   You sound like Jacob, but I know you are Esau because I can feel your rough skin and I would know that smell anywhere. You must be Esau. Now, my son, I give you my blessing that you may prosper always. You shall be the head of this family and they must do as you say. I curse anyone who harms you and I bless anyone who helps you.

Narrator   And that is how Jacob received the blessing meant for Esau. Now, when Esau found out what happened, he was very upset, so Jacob ran for his life and left the land of Canaan to live in another land. There, Jacob married, had many sons, and grew very rich. Years later, he returned to Canaan and made peace with his brother Esau. Jacob did become the leader of his family as he was meant to be.

Gideon and the Midianites
(Adapted from Judges 7)

Characters   Gideon   Props: Horn
                Angel   Sheepskin or other piece of fur
                Israelites
                Midianites   Background scenery: Picture of cave
                Narrator   Picture of a tent
                Voice of God

Scene One: In the cave

Narrator   It was in the days of the Judges and the people of Israel were having many problems. The Midianites crossed the Jordan River and destroyed the farms of the Israelites and sent them fleeing into caves in the mountains. Finally, God took pity on the Israelites and sent an angel to the young soldier, Gideon.

Angel   Don't be gloomy, Gideon. God is with you and the Israelites.

Gideon   With me? With us? You have got to be kidding. If God is with us, why are we hiding out in the caves? Looks to me like God is with the other guys.

Angel   Uh, uh, no way! God is with you, all right. Now go out and save your nation from the Midianites.

Gideon   Me? You just can't mean me. Do you realize that I am the weakest member of my family and my family is the least important in the whole tribe of Israel? That puts me way down on the popularity polls. I can't do this.

Angel   You can do it because God has chosen you and will be with you.

Gideon   This is wild! I can't believe any of this, but you do look like an angel, all right. Well, if God really wants me, I have to have more evidence before I stick *my* neck out. Tell you what. I'll just spread this sheepskin out on the floor. If it is wet with dew tomorrow morning and the floor is dry, then I will be sure.

Angel   You've got yourself a deal.

Narrator   And so, Gideon, still full of doubt, spread the sheepskin on the floor and settled down for the night. The next day...

Gideon	It's wet! It's really wet and everything else is dry. That angel was for real. O.K., God. I'll do it! Where's my horn? *(Blows horn and soldier puppets appear.)* Wow! Good turnout! Over a thousand soldiers! O.K. soldiers, line up, right face, single file, 1, 2, 3...
Voice of God	Oh, Gideon?
Gideon	*(looking around.)* God? Is that you, God?
Voice of God	You will not need all those troops. I want all to know it was I who won the battle for Israel and not a huge army. Just ask which soldiers are frightened and send them home.
Narrator	Gideon did as God asked and sent one half the army away.
Gideon	O.K., soldiers, line up, single file, right face, 1, 2, 3....
Voice of God	Oh, Gideon?
Gideon	*(impatiently looking around)* Now what?
Voice of God	Still too many. You must put them to another test. Take them to the river to drink. The soldiers who drink directly from the stream should be sent away. Those who drink from water cupped in their hands will be your army.
Gideon	Are you sure? There won't be many left.
Voice of God	Do as I say, Gideon. I will be with you. Trust me.
Gideon	O.K., soldiers, is anybody thirsty? Let's take a break. To the stream, everyone.
Narrator	Again Gideon did as God asked and when the troops were finished drinking only 300 remained.
Gideon	Unbelievable! 300 left to defeat the powerful Midianite army. But God is with me. I must believe that. O.K., soldiers, now here is our plan. *(Puppets huddle together and leave the stage.)*

Scene Two: In front of enemy tents

(As this scene opens, the Midianite puppets are sleeping in various positions.)

Narrator	Now, Gideon may not have been a brilliant general, but he was no fool either. In a very sneaky move, he and the Israelites attacked the Midianites in the middle of the night. Their attack was totally unexpected.
	(Gideon and the Israelite puppets act out the following scene.)
	Those 300 men blew trumpets and carried on, making such a racket that they sounded like a huge army. The Midianites awoke all confused and scared and started fighting with each other because it was dark and they could not see. It really was a mess inside the enemy tents and Gideon and his men took full advantage of the situation. They chased those Midianites back across the Jordan River. The Israelites were then able to return home.
Soldiers	Let's hear it for Gideon. Hip, Hip, Hooray!
Soldier	Be our king and rule over us, Gideon. You deserve to be king.
Gideon	I cannot be your king. Your king is the Lord God. Go and worship God.
Narrator	And so the people of Israel returned to their homes. Gideon served as a judge and always reminded the Israelites to trust in God, just as this story reminds us that God is always with us even when we feel alone and afraid.

Joseph Forgives
(Based on the story in Genesis 37 and 42)

Characters: Narrator   Levi   Props: Bags of grain
           Joseph   Judah   Goblet
           Steward   Dan
           Rueben   Gad   Background scenery: Palace
           Simeon   Asher
           Isaachar   Benjamin
           Zebulum   Naphtali

Narrator Sometimes when others hurt us or are nasty to us or say mean things to us, it's very hard to forgive them. Jesus taught us to do that, to forgive those people who hurt us. Long before Jesus lived, there was one of God's people who also taught us a lesson about forgiveness. His name was Joseph and.... Well, I'll let his brothers tell the story.

Rueben You see, the problem started when Joseph was born. Our father, Jacob, had several wives, which was O.K. in our time. Father really liked Joseph's mother better than his other wives, so that made Joseph special.

Simeon Yeah, he was really spoiled, got treated the best. It really bugged us.

Levi Finally, near his 17th birthday, Father gave him a really special gift: a beautiful coat of many colors! We all wanted one like it.

Judah But, of course, no coats for us. We just had to keep on working in the fields and wearing the same old clothes.

Isaachar We just couldn't take it anymore.

Zebulum That's when we got the idea to get rid of Joseph.

Dan One day when we were out in the field, we sneaked up on him and ripped off his coat. Rueben would not let us *really* get rid of him.

Rueben It was my idea to just throw him down the well. So we did.

Napthali	Later that day, a caravan came by and Judah had a better idea.
Judah	Well, Joseph was our brother. I did not feel very good about letting him die in the well. "Let us just sell him. We can get rid of him and even get paid for it," I said. So we did!
Asher	Then, we killed a goat and smeared blood all over Joseph's fancy coat. We told father that Joseph had been torn to pieces by a wild beast.
Gad	Father took the news very badly and was really sad.
Simeon	In the meantime, Joseph was alive and well in Egypt. God had a special plan for Joseph and after many exciting adventures, Joseph ended up with an important job in the court of the Pharaoh.
Isaachar	In fact, Joseph was the number two man in the whole country. He had warned the Pharaoh that after seven years of plenty with lots of food and good crops, there would be seven years of famine with lots of hunger and no crops.
Napthali	The Pharaoh ordered the warehouses to be filled with grain, so Egypt was well prepared for the famine.
Zebulum	That's when we met up with our brother Joseph again.
	(Brothers leave stage as Joseph and steward enter.)
Joseph	Well, steward, what is on the schedule today?
Steward	More people from other countries, Governor. Here are ten gentlemen to see you. They need food for their hungry families back in Canaan.
	(Brothers enter and bow to Joseph.)
Joseph	*(surprised)* Ahh, and what may I do for you gentlemen?
Rueben	Please, sir, sell us some grain. We all have families and a father and a younger brother at home.
Joseph	*(thoughtfully)* Hmmm. You look like spies to me. I will sell you no food until I see this younger brother. Then I will know you are not spies. Bring him to me. *(Brothers leave and Joseph bows his head and sobs.)* My brothers. *(Joseph and steward leave stage.)*

Narrator	The brothers traveled back to Canaan and told their father that the only way to get food was to take Benjamin to Egypt. Jacob's heart was broken again, but he had no choice. His people were hungry. He had to let Benjamin go.
Steward	*(entering behind Joseph)* Governor, sir, the gentlemen from Canaan have returned.
Joseph	So, you have kept your word.
Judah	Yes, sir. This is Benjamin, our younger brother.
Joseph	*(shaking hands)* How do you do, Benjamin? And tell me about your father. Is he in good health?
Benjamin	Yes, sir. He is alive and well.
Joseph	Good. Good. Well, come and have a meal. You have kept your word and so I shall keep mine. *(Puppets leave stage.)*
Narrator	While they were eating, Joseph had his brothers' sacks filled with grain, but in Benjamin's sack, he hid a silver goblet. The next day, the brothers left to go back to Canaan. *(Puppets enter.)* They had not traveled far when Joseph sent his steward after them.
Steward	Whoa, there. Stop, I say! We have a little problem here.
Dan	A problem?
Steward	A matter of a missing silver goblet. I'll need to search your bags.
Rueben	Certainly. Certainly. You will not find the silver in our bags.
Steward	*(Searches through bags and finds the goblet in Benjamin's bags.)* Ah hah! Here it is!
Zebulum	How did it get there? In Benjamin's bag? Oh, no! He wouldn't steal anything.
Steward	You will have to speak to my master about this.
Narrator	So they all returned to the governor's court to beg for mercy.
Joseph	Hmmm. Hmmm. Well, there is good news and there is bad news. The bad news first. My goblet was found in Benjamin's

29

bag, so he will have to stay here and be my slave. The good news is that the rest of you may go free.

Judah Please, sir. Please understand. If you keep Benjamin here our father will die of sorrow. He has already lost one son whom he loved very much. He just couldn't take this. Please, sir, let me take Benjamin's place. I'll be your slave. Please let him go free.

Joseph *(softly and slowly)* I am your brother Joseph, the brother you sold to the caravan. God has led me here and blessed me. I have helped men and women and saved their lives. Now I will save yours. *(Hugs Benjamin.)* Benjamin, dear brother.

Asher *(bowing)* Forgive us, Joseph. We are sorry. Please forgive us.

Joseph You do not need to bow to me. Of course I forgive you. You are my brothers. Now, go back to Canaan and bring our father here to Egypt because this famine will go on for another five years. Bring your flocks and families and everything you own.

Narrator Then Joseph hugged each of his brothers and forgave them. They all wept for the joy and the love that filled their hearts. For no matter how much his brothers had hurt him, Joseph loved them and was willing to forgive them. Never forget that God forgives us in the same way.

Moses and the Burning Bush
(Based on the story in Exodus 3)

Characters: Voice of God   Props: Bush
                  Moses   Staff
                  Aaron
                  Narrator   Background scenery: Mountain

Narrator   Many years passed after the Israelites went to live with Joseph in Egypt. There was a new Pharaoh and he was not a nice fellow. The Israelites were made slaves to help build the mighty pyramids and temples in Egypt, but God heard their cries of suffering and their prayers for help. God remembered the promise made to Abraham years before.

Moses   *(enters)* Over here, sheep. Lots of grass around. *(looking around)* It really is peaceful here in Midian. I'm not really sorry I had to run away from Egypt because I tried to save that Israelite slave. I like it here. It is beautiful.

(A bush made from fluorescent paper appears, or a light could shine from behind a paper bush.)

Wow, what is that? The bush is on fire. I'd better throw some water on it. *(pretending to throw water on the bush)* This is weird! Those are flames, all right, but the bush is not burning. I must be dreaming. *(shaking Moses)* Wake up, Moses! Maybe it was that taco I had for lunch.

Voice of God   Moses. Moses.

Moses   Hey, what's that?

Voice of God   Here I am?

Moses   Who's there?

Voice of God   Don't come any closer. Take off your shoes for you are standing on holy ground.

Moses   But who are you?

Voice of God   I am the God of Abraham, the God of Isaac, and the God of Jacob.

Moses	O.K., I believe you. There, my shoes are off, but I'm afraid to look at you, God.
Voice of God	Don't be afraid, Moses.
Moses	But God, why did you decide to come disguised as a burning bush?
Voice of God	To get your attention. It worked, didn't it?
Moses	It sure did.
Voice of God	You see, Moses, I have seen the suffering of my people in Egypt. I have heard them crying out to me and I have come to rescue them and guide them to Canaan.
Moses	Great idea! You should have done that years ago, but you should be telling them, not me.
Voice of God	You are the one I need to tell because I want you to go to Pharaoh and tell him to let my people go.
Moses	*(in disbelief)* Me?
Voice of God	Yes, you, and then after you do that, you are to bring the children of Israel safely out of Egypt.
Moses	But why did you pick me out for this job? And it really is a *big* job!
Voice of God	Don't be afraid, Moses. I will help you.
Moses	*(sarcastically)* Well, that's a relief!
Voice of God	And when you have brought your people out of Egypt, please bring them right back to this mountain to worship.
Moses	If I do this thing, and I'm not saying I will, what will I say to the Israelites when they ask who sent me?
Voice of God	Tell them that the God of their ancestors sent you, the God of Abraham, Isaac, and Jacob. My name is the God Yahweh.
Moses	I don't think they will listen to me.
Voice of God	What is in your hand, Moses?

Moses	My shepherd's staff, a stick of wood. Why do you ask?
Voice of God	Throw it on the ground.
Moses	*(Throws stick and jumps back.)* Ugh! A snake! Ugh!
Voice of God	Pick it up by the tail, Moses.
Moses	Do I have to?
Voice of God	Moses...
Moses	O.K., O.K. *(picking up "snake")* Hey! It's my stick again! How did you do that?
Voice of God	Put your hand inside your robe, Moses. Now, pull it out.
Moses	*(Puts hand in robe and takes it out.)* Oh, no! My hand is all white and covered with sores. I must have some kind of terrible disease!
Voice of God	Put your hand back inside your robe, Moses. Now, pull it out again.
Moses	Wow! It's O.K. I'm normal again. I can't believe it!
Voice of God	I am giving you these two signs to prove to people that you are my messenger and I have sent you to help them. Now, go down to Egypt, Moses, and bring the Israelites out of slavery and into freedom.
Moses	God, I'm not the guy you are looking for. I have never been able to speak without a stutter. The people would never be able to listen to me.
Voice of God	Who do you think makes a person to speak well, hear well, or see clearly? I do that. Trust me, Moses, I will help you when you speak and I will tell you what to say.
Moses	No, Lord. Please send someone else. I can't do this.
Voice of God	Sure you can because you will have help. You have a brother named Aaron and he will do the speaking for you. He is on his way to meet you.
Moses	He is coming to meet me?

Voice of God   Yes, and I will help you both and tell you what to do. You can tell Aaron what to say and he will speak to the people for you.

Narrator   So, Moses went home, packed his bag and said goodbye to his family. With his staff in his hand, he set out toward Egypt to meet his brother Aaron. Moses was very happy to see his brother again and he told Aaron all that God had told him. Then Moses and Aaron went into Egypt and met with leaders of the Israelites. Aaron told the people that God had sent Moses, and Moses showed them God's signs. The Israelites believed God had heard their prayers and would set them free, so they kneeled down in praise and thanksgiving to God.

Solomon's Decision
(Based on the story in 1 Kings 3: 16-28)

Characters: Narrator   Props: Baby
                      Voice of God   Sword
                      King Solomon
                      First Woman
                      Second Woman
                      Guard   Background scenery: Palace

Narrator   Solomon became king of Israel when he was still a young man. He wanted to be a good king and he prayed to God for help.

Scene One

Solomon   *(sleeping soundly and snoring)* *Zzzzzzz. Zzzzzzzz. Zzzzzzzz.*

Voice of God   I will help you Solomon, but what do you want from me?

Solomon   I want to be great like my father. He was old and wise when he died, but I am young and have no experience. Give me wisdom so I can judge between good and evil. Give me the skill to listen so I may learn from others. Give me eyes to see clearly so that I may understand. Give me goodness and honesty so I may serve you.

Voice of God   Solomon, I am so happy with you. You did not ask for riches or for a long life or for the blood of your enemies. What you asked for, you will receive and much more, too. For as long as people live, they will praise the wisdom and judgment of Solomon.

Narrator   Solomon got to put his new gifts to use right away. Two women came to the palace to see the king and get him to settle an argument.

Scene Two

(King enters followed by a guard and two women. One woman lays a baby at the feet of King Solomon.)

Guard   Your majesty, both these women claim to be the mother of this child.

First Woman	Your majesty, I am the mother of this child.
Second Woman	No, she is not. I am. Both of our babies were born on the same night but her baby was born dead.
First Woman	No, your majesty. This woman is lying. Her baby is the one who was born dead. This baby is mine. Please say it is mine!
Second Woman	It's mine!
First Woman	No, it's mine!
Second Woman	It's mine, I say!
Solomon	*(pauses thoughtfully)* Hmm. Hmm. Which one of you is telling the truth?
First Woman	I am, your majesty. While I slept, she came in and stole my baby and put her dead one in its place.
Second Woman	You are lying!
Solomon	Well now, let me see. Hmmm. Hmmm. One child cannot belong to two mothers. One of you is lying. Which one is it?
First Woman	I'm telling the truth.
Second Woman	Me too. She is the one who is lying.
Solomon	*(to the guard)* Bring me a sword. *(to the audience)* God has brought these two women to me and each says she is the mother of this child. Each wants me to say she is the child's mother. Since they both want the child, each shall have half of it. The child shall be cut into two pieces.
First Woman	*(Rushes to the king.)* No! Don't kill him. Please don't kill him. Let her have my son.
Solomon	*(to the guard)* Put away your sword. Do not hurt this child. *(to the audience)* Now, we know which one is the real mother. One of these women wants only her satisfaction. But the true mother would bring misery on herself before she would allow her child to be hurt. *(to the first woman)* Here is your son, and teach him to follow God's commandments.

Narrator	So, Solomon did indeed use the gifts God had given him. He listened, he saw clearly, and he used wisdom to judge between good and evil. Even if we are not the wisest king who ever lived, we can still use these same gifts to live the life God would have us live.

Elijah's Contest with the Priests of Baal
(Based on the story in 1 Kings 17 and 18)

Characters: Elijah
 King Ahab
 Obadiah
 One of the people
 Israelites
 Narrator

Props: Altar for priests
 Simple altar for Elizjah

Background scenery: At the palace
 At Mt. Carmel

Narrator   There are several exciting stories in the Bible about Elijah, the prophet. This is the story of Elijah and the priests of Baal. King Ahab and Queen Jezebel ruled Israel. They worshiped Baal and this really upset Elijah.

Scene One: At the palace

King Ahab   There has been no rain here for three years and that means the land is burning up, and that means no crops, and that means hunger everywhere— famine.

Obadiah   I know, sir, but what are we to do?

King Ahab   I'm not sure, but I know that crazy prophet, Elijah, has something to do with this. He has been gone for three years and that is how long it has been since we had rain. Well, for now I want you to go out and look for hidden springs so we can help keep people and animals alive.

Obadiah   Yes sir, I'm on my way. *(He leaves.)*

Narrator   Obadiah went out to look for water, and on his way he met Elijah. The prophet told Obadiah to go tell the king he had returned. The king then sent for Elijah.

Elijah   *(enters)* You wanted to see me?

King Ahab   Enough is enough. I know you are the cause of this weather problem. You did this to get even with me. With no rain, we have no crops and with no crops, everyone is hungry. *You* are to blame.

Elijah   Me? Me? You think I am to blame?

King Ahab	Don't play dumb with me, Elijah. You know you are to blame.
Elijah	Hey, king, don't blame me. It is because of *your* wickedness that this mess is happening.
King Ahab	Me, wicked?
Elijah	You and your false god, Baal.
King Ahab	Not that complaint again. People are starving here and you keep whining about that. Now what about this weather problem?
Elijah	The rains will come back. But first, you and all your priests have to meet me on Mt. Carmel.
Narrator	Ahab really had no choice, so the priests of Baal were ordered to go to Mt. Carmel. Thousands of people followed to see what was happening.

Scene Two: Mt. Carmel

Elijah	*(to the audience)* O.K., folks. How much longer are you going to sit on the fence? Either Baal is the true God or the God Yahweh is.
One of the People	He is asking? He doesn't know?
Elijah	Well, I say God is. Now here are 450 priests who say Baal is. So, let us settle this matter once and for all. We will both prepare a bull for sacrifice. We will cut it up and put it on the wood. Then comes the test. We will each call our God to light the fire. The God who answers by fire is the true God. What do you think?
People	Yeah! Yeah! Yeah!
Narrator	So, the priests of Baal built an altar, killed the bull, and put it with the wood on top of the altar. *(Puppets pretend to do all this.)*
Priests	*(dancing around altar and singing chants)* Baal, Baal, answer us. Send us fire, Baal, Baal.
Elijah	*(teasing them)* Call louder. Baal can't hear you.
Priests	*(dancing wildly and singing)* Baal, Baal, You are the best.

	Send us fire So we win the test!
Elijah	He still can't hear you.
Priests	*(yelling wildly)* Baaal! Baaaaaal! Baaaaal!
Elijah	Well, it appears that Baal is either not there or is out to lunch. My turn!
Narrator	So Elijah built an altar to God and put the bull on the wood.
Elijah	And to show you how sure I am about who is really God, I will make the job harder. I'll just pour some water on this. *(Pretending to pour water on fire.)*
One of the People	No! He must be crazy!

(Elijah pours water on fire a second time.)

Obadiah	He is doing it again!

(Elijah pours water on fire a third time.)

King Ahab	And again! He *is* crazy!
Elijah	Now, God of Abraham, God of Isaac, God of Israel. Let the people see that you alone are God. *(Elijah stands quietly.)*

(Fire appears—may be a flashlight or orange paper pushed up from the back of the altar.)

People	Flames! Look! Ahhh!
King Ahab	It happened. The bull is burning!
Obadiah	The wood is burning!
People	The stones are burning!
Priests	The water is burning!
People	Elijah's God is the true God!
Elijah	Not my God, *our God!* The God of us all.

People   The Lord is God. The Lord is God.

Elijah   Seize the priests for they have brought great evil. Take them away. *(turning to the King)* And you, king, go home and have dinner, for I hear the sound of rain.

Narrator   And that is the story of how Elijah, a prophet of great courage, won the contest with the priests of Baal. He was not afraid of losing because his faith in God was so strong that Elijah was willing to stand alone.

Shadrach, Meschach, and Abedne...Who?

(Based on the story in Daniel 1)

Characters: Narrator   Messenger

                  King Nebuchadnezzar   Guard

                  Shadrachst   Israelite

                  Meschach   2nd Israelite

                  Abednego   3rd Israelite

                  Wiseman

Scene One: In the palace court

Narrator   Long ago, the people of Israel were captured by their enemies, carried to other lands, and made to be slaves. It was a sad time in their history because the Israelites were homesick and, even worse, they were forced to bow down to other gods. In the country of Babylon, King Nebuchadnezzar used the slaves to build a big, golden statue. Then he called all the people together.

Guard   People of every land and language! The king has ordered you to come here to worship the golden statue. This will be a sign. When the trumpets toot, everyone should fall on their knees. Bow down till your forehead touches the ground and worship the statue. Anyone who does not will be thrown into the furnace and be burned to death.

1st Israelite   What does this mean?

2nd Israelite   I'm afraid to ask.

3rd Israelite   O.K. O.K. I'm down.

1st Israelite   Great King Nebuchadnezzar, you really scare us. Don't burn us. Have mercy on us.

2nd Israelite   Yes, don't throw us in the oven. We will gladly be your slaves.

All   Hail King! Hail, statue!

King   Good. Good. I am glad you approve.

Wiseman   Bad news, King. Not everyone does approve. Didn't you say everyone had to fall down and worship the statue?

King	Yes.
Wiseman	And anyone who does not will be thrown into the furnace?
King	Yes.
Wiseman	Well, there are three Jews who are not doing that!
King	Really? Bring them to me.
Wiseman	*(Comes back with three others.)* Here they are.
King	What do you call yourselves?
Shadrach	Shadrach.
Meschach	Meschach.
Abednego	And Abednego.
King	You seem to have a little problem getting down on your knees.
Shadrach	Not really. We just do not believe in your god.
Meschach	So we are not going to bow down to that silly statue.
Abednego	And you can't make us.
King	That does it. Into the fire!
Guard	O.K., you guys. Let's go.
King	*(Calls after them.)* Put extra wood on the fire. Make it even hotter.
	(The furnace is not seen. Puppets pretend to look below stage at the furnace.)
1st Israelite	Oh, no! I can't look.
2nd Israelite	It's awful. The flames are high.
3rd Israelite	Are they burned up yet?
1st Israelite	Not yet, they're walking around down there.

King	Hey, down there! Hey, Guard! Didn't you throw those three guys into the furnace?
Guard	Yes, your majesty, and they are still in there.
King	Well, who is that fourth guy I see down there.
1st Israelite	Wow! There are four.
King	I see four men. I see them clearly. They are walking around and that fourth guy...he looks like an angel. *(Looks up.)* No, that can't be.
2nd Israelite	But it is. There is an angel in there with them.
3rd Israelite	And the fire isn't even touching them!
King	*(thoughtfully)* It is true. It is true. *(loudly)* Come out, you servants of God.
Shadrach, Meschach, Abednego	*(popping up from stage below)* Here we are!
1st Israelite	They are not even pink.
2nd Israelite	Not a hair on their head is burned.
3rd Israelite	They don't even smell like smoke.
King	Blessed be the God of Shadrach, Meschach, and Abednego for their God is the true God.
Narrator	And that is the story of the three brave persons who refused to turn away from God. They chose to be faithful even if it meant death, but God protected them and kept them safe. Their strong faith made others believe in God.

The Sad Story of Job
(Based on the story in the book of Job)

Characters: Narrator   Background scenery: A country scene
                    Job   with some trees,
                    Voice of God   hills, and flowers
                    Satan
                    Servant
                    Friend

Narrator Once upon a time long ago in the land of Uz there lived a man named Job. Now, this man was truly unbelievable. Some said he lived a charmed life because everything about him was nearly perfect. Job was very rich and owned cattle, sheep, camels, and much land. He had many servants to care for him. He had fine sons and daughters who were polite and well-behaved and always on the honor roll. Even more unbelievable was his goodness, for Job was truly a good man who always obeyed God's law and walked in God's holy ways. One day as the angels gathered around God, Satan popped in for a visit. *(Satan pops up.)*

Voice of God Well, hello there. Haven't seen you around for awhile. Where have you been?

Satan Oh, here and there.

Voice of God Have you noticed my good and faithful servant, Job? Now, there is a good man.

Satan He is only good because *you* make it so easy for him.

Voice of God I beg your pardon?

Satan Take away Job's rewards and he will curse your name.

Voice of God Very well. Take them away and we shall see, but do not touch Job himself.

(Satan leaves. Servant and Job appear.)

Servant Mister Job, I have, uh, some bad news.

45

Job Yes?

Servant Well, we just got a call from the police department and I'm sorry to have to report that some nasty robbers carried off all your animals last night. All your cattle, sheep, and camels are gone.

Job Oh my! Well, no problem. I still have my wealth, my land, my family, and my health. *(Servant leaves, then returns.)*

Servant Uh, Mr. Job?

Job Yes?

Servant I'm sorry to tell you that the man from the bank just called to say that the bank was robbed and you lost all your money.

Job Oh my! No problem. I still have my land, my family, and my health. *(Servant leaves, then returns.)*

Servant More bad news, Mr. Job. The man from the Income Tax Department just called. It is time to pay your taxes and since you do not have any animals or money, the government is taking your land to pay the taxes.

Job Oh, my! This *is* getting worse. Well, no problem. I still have my children and my health. *(Servant leaves, then returns.)*

Servant Uh, Mr. Job? I have terrible news. Your children were having dinner at your oldest son's home when a big wind came up, the roof fell in, and I'm sorry to report that all your children are dead.

Job Oh, no! Oh, no! I can't take this. My children! Oh, no!

Satan *(from the side of the stage)* Ah hah! Now he will curse God.

Job Well, I came into this world with nothing and I shall leave it with nothing. The Lord gave me what I had and it was all the Lord's to take away. Blessed is the Lord.

Satan Rats!

Voice of God You see, I told you Job was a good man.

Satan Well, that wasn't much of a test. You would not even let me touch him. I'll bet if his body is in real pain, Job will curse you.

Voice of God Go ahead, but spare his life.

Satan Zap!

Job What are all these sores on my body? Yech! They're getting worse. Ouch! They hurt!

Friend Don't complain, Job. Just ask God what you did wrong. He will forgive you and you will get better.

Job I did nothing wrong. Anyway, I don't know how to reach God to argue my case.

Friend Shocking! You can't argue with God. All human beings are sinners.

Job I know as much about God as you do. God made me and he knows I am innocent. I need a fair trial.

Friend Control yourself, Job. God *is* angry. Mend your ways.

Narrator Job prayed to God and argued his case. God listened to Job because Job was such a good man. Job never blamed God for his problems and he certainly never cursed God. He just begged for mercy.

Voice of God Stand up little Job. I am here. Come with me and let me show you our world. *(to the friend)* As for you, I am really angry. You were mean to your friend and offered no help to Job at all. Job did nothing wrong. Don't you know a good man when you see him?

Satan *(from the side of the stage)* Rats! Rats! Rats!

Narrator Job was so happy to see his God. He understood that sometimes people suffer, but when that happens they should not curse God. They should pray and reach out to God just as Job did. God gave Job back his perfect health, and more children, and made him twice as rich as he was before. Job lived a long and a happy life.

Queen Esther's Secret
(Based on the story in the book of Esther)

Characters: Narrator   Background scenery: Palace
                      King Xerxes
                      Haman
                      Mordecai
                      Esther

Narrator   Once upon a time there was a great king who ruled over Persia and all the land from India to Africa. His name was Xerxes and he was so rich and powerful he could have whatever he wanted. Now King Xerxes had a disagreement with his queen. He became so angry that he kicked her out of his kingdom. Then he held a beauty contest so he could select a new queen. The contestants had to spend a whole year learning how to make themselves lovely enough to please the king. At the end of the year, the king picked Esther, the most beautiful of all, and made her his queen. What the king did not know was that Esther was Jewish and not Persian. The Jews were being held captive in Persia so they were looked upon as lower class citizens. Esther's parents were dead and, before she was queen, she had been cared for by her Uncle Mordecai. And now our story begins....

Mordecai   *(Enters with Queen Esther.)* Hello, Esther.

Esther   Hello, Uncle. I am so glad to see you. How are you?

Mordecai   Well, I am fine, Esther, but I am very concerned. I overheard the two palace gatekeepers planning to kill the king.

Esther   No!

Mordecai   I am afraid it is true and I wanted to warn you about this.

Esther   Oh, thank you, Uncle. I shall tell the king at once.

(Mordecai leaves and the king enters.)

King   Oh, there you are, my beautiful queen.

Esther   Your majesty, may I have a word with you?

King   Of course.

Esther   I have learned of a terrible plot to kill you.

King   Oh? And who are the scoundrels who plan to do this?

Esther   Come close and let me whisper their names.

King   *(in disbelief)* No! Well, that is the end of them. *(calls)* Guards! Go get the front gatekeepers. Take them to the gallows and hang them till they are dead. That will teach them a lesson. They planned to kill me— can you believe it?

Guard   Yes, sir. I'll take care of them, sir.

(All puppets leave stage.)

Narrator   Sometime later, the king hired a new adviser named Haman. He was very bright and a good worker but he had one problem— he hated Jews! He hated them with a passion. Most of all, he hated Mordecai, because Mordecai would not kneel to him.

Haman   *(Enters with the King.)* Your majesty, we have this problem. The Jews are becoming real pests.

King   Oh, now, they can't be all that bad.

Haman   They are! They refuse to bow to us and they dishonor you because they still believe in that silly God of theirs, the God of Abraham, Isaac, and some other fellow. These Jews are *your* subjects. If they get away with this disobedience, your own people will soon get unruly.

King   Hmmm. Maybe you are right. Well, how would you fix this problem.

Haman   Kill every Jew in Persia. Too many Jews here anyhow. It's getting too crowded. We could do it on the feast day of Pur. It would set a good example for your subjects. It will teach them to be loyal and obedient.

King   O.K. Do it! *(Puppets leave.)*

Narrator   When Esther learned of Haman's order, she was afraid for her people. What could she do? If she tried to talk to the king, her life would surely be in danger. Finally, she put on her royal robes and risked her life by going to the king when he didn't even send for her.

Esther   *(Enters with the King.)* Your majesty, sir.

King   Esther, you become more beautiful every time I see you. You have made me so happy. You may have anything you want. Speak and it is yours.

Esther   Please have dinner with me tonight in my room and bring Haman with you. *(King and Esther leave.)*

Narrator   The king was happy to have dinner with his beautiful queen, even if his adviser did have to join them.

King   *(King, Esther, and Haman enter.)* You look even more beautiful tonight than you did today, my queen. I am really in love. I want you to be happy. I will grant any wish you have. You can even have half my kingdom.

Esther   No, that is not what I want. Do you remember when I told you about the plot to kill you?

King   Yes.

Esther   Well, the one who told me about the plot was my Uncle Mordecai.

King   He certainly must be thanked for doing that and we must honor him, give him a medal or a plaque. Take care of that, Haman.

Esther   Your majesty, Mordecai is a Jew.

King   Is that so?

Esther   *(softly)* And so am I.

King   No!

Esther   Haman wants to kill Mordecai and me and all our people. We are innocent people trying to live in peace while we are captives here. Please save our lives. We don't want to die.

King   *(calls loudly)* Guards. Come at once!

Haman   Not very smart, queenie. You should have kept your little secret.

Now you have had it.

King   *(to Haman)* No, my friend. You have had it. How could you think I could destroy my brave, beautiful queen or Mordecai, the man who saved my life? These people ARE innocent and more loyal than you will ever be. *(Guard enters.) (to Guard)* Take this miserable worm away and hang him until he is dead. *Guard takes Haman away.) (to Esther)* Come here, my darling. No one will harm you.

Narrator   Then the king made Mordecai the number one adviser. The Feast of Pur did take place, but no Jew was killed. Today, this holy day is called Purim and it is remembered as a time when the Jewish people overcame the hatred of their enemies because of the courageous act of Queen Esther. For she could have kept silent and been safe. Instead, she risked her own life, told the truth, and saved her people.

Daniel and the Big Cats
(Based on the story in the book of Daniel)

Characters: Narrator   Background scenery: Palace
                 King Darius   Front of lion's den
                 Department Head
                 Daniel

Narrator   Even though the Israelites were made to live in Babylon for many years, some still remained faithful to their God. The prophet Daniel was one of those people who never stopped believing in God. He preached about God and about the messiah who would come later. Of course, Daniel had to be a little careful talking about this if he wanted to keep his job in the king's court. King Darius really liked Daniel so he promoted him and made Daniel a big boss over 120 little department heads. Some of these department heads became jealous and tried to figure out some neat way to get rid of Daniel.

Scene One: Palace

Department Head   *(Enters stage, following King Darius.)* Your Majesty, we have a little problem.

King Darius   We do?

Department Head   Yes. Daniel. He has to go.

King Darius   Go? Go where?

Department Head   Into the lion's den.

King Darius   Again? Are you still picking on him?

Department Head   Your Majesty, he is breaking your laws again.

King Darius   *(annoyed)* Let's see. You griped because Daniel eats only veggies with no meat....And then you griped because you didn't like the dreams he had....And then you griped....

Department Head	Well, Your Majesty, you have to admit he is weird! But this is serious. Persian law says we must worship you, but Daniel doesn't.
King Darius	He doesn't?
Department Head	No, Daniel falls on his knees, facing Jerusalem, three times a day.
King Darius	Well, he's homesick. Can't blame him for that.
Department Head	But he prays to the Lord God and *that* makes him a *traitor*. The penalty for traitors is to be thrown to the lions.
King Darius	But I can't do that. I love Daniel. He is good and honest and he works so hard.
Department Head	There is no other way. If you do not punish Daniel, your subjects will begin to do as they please. Here is the death warrant. Sign on the dotted line.
King Darius	*(sighing)* If I must, I must. Go and do what you would have me do.
	(Department Head leaves.)
Narrator	So the King went to his room to pray. He could not sleep at all, for he knew that Daniel was being torn to pieces by the lions. The next morning King Darius got up and went down to the lion's den.

Scene Two: By the lion's den

King Darius	It's so quiet. It must be all over for Daniel. *(calls)* Daniel, Daniel, servant of the living God. Are you still alive?
Daniel	Shhh. Yes, I am here.
King Darius	*(yelling)* You are! You are alive!
Daniel	Yes, but please don't yell. You will awaken my furry friends here.

King Darius   Because you trusted God with your heart and your soul, God saved you. Come out, my friend, and walk with me.

(Department head enters and is surprised.)

King Darius   *(to the department head)* And you! You tried to destroy this good man. You are fired!*(to the audience)* Now listen to my proclamation:
Peace be with you!
Let all nations honor the God of Daniel,
Who has saved him even from the lions.
For this is the Almighty,
The living God
And God's kingdom shall never end.

Miracle of the Loaves and Fishes
(Based on the story in John 6)

Characters: Narrator
           Jesus
           Andrew
           Phillip
           Peter
           People on hillside

Props: Bread (paper)
      Fish (paper)
      Baskets (paper)

Background scenery: Hillside by a lake

Narrator As Jesus traveled through Galilee preaching and teaching, many people gathered to hear him.

Jesus We have been traveling and preaching for many days and we are getting tired. Come, let us go to a quiet place where we can rest our minds and our bodies.

Peter But where is there such a place? You are so popular now that there are people everywhere who come to see and hear you.

Jesus Let us go out in the boat. It's calm and peaceful on the Sea of Galilee.

Narrator So, Jesus went out in a boat but he could not really rest for he was filled with love and pity for all those people who waited on the shore. They seemed so lost, like sheep without a shepherd. Finally, Jesus steered the boat back to shore.

Jesus Come, everyone. Let us go and sit awhile. I have some special parables to share with you. *(Jesus and the people go and sit at one end of the stage.)*

Narrator Even though he was very tired, Jesus spent the whole day with the people. Soon it was evening,then it was morning, then the next evening, then morning, and finally evening again. Three days later...

Andrew It is time to send these people away so we can go and eat.

Phillip Sounds like a great idea. I'm really getting hungry.

Peter Me, too. Let's go tell the master. *(Puppets approach Jesus.)*

Andrew	Master, it's getting late. We should send these people home.
Phillip	We've been here for three days.
Peter	And some of the people have a long way to travel.
Jesus	Then we must feed them.
Peter	*(in disbelief)* What?
Jesus	We will give them food.
Andrew	You can't be serious. We can't feed all these people.
Jesus	Then we will buy food for them.
Phillip	We would need at least 200 pieces of silver to buy enough bread to fill all these people.
Andrew	Just look around. There must be 5,000 people here.
Jesus	*(tiredly)* Well, how much food can we gather here?
	(Puppets look around.)
Phillip	One little guy gave us five barley loaves and two fish. He is willing to share it, but that is all we have.
Peter	*(sarcastically)* Great! That should feed about six people.
Jesus	*(quietly)* Tell everyone to sit down. Have them sit in small groups so it will be easier for you to pass the food around.
Peter	*(grumbling)* That should take about two minutes.
Jesus	*(Takes bread and fish and looks up to heaven.)* Thank you, God, for this food. Amen. Now, I will break the bread and divide the fish. Then you can pass it around.
Narrator	Everyone there was very hungry, so they began to eat. They ate and ate and still there was plenty more. They ate and ate until everyone was stuffed.
Andrew	I can't believe it! We fed 5,000 people with two fish and five little barley loaves. Amazing!

Phillip And there is enough left over to fill 12 baskets.

Peter Yeh. How did that happen?

Andrew It's a miracle! An amazing miracle!

Phillip The people are happy because you taught them about love and forgiveness and they are satisfied because you gave them bread. They are at peace.

Jesus And now let us go up into the hills where we can rest and pray together.

Pentecost - It's Strange!

(Based on a story in Acts 2)

Characters: Disciple 1
Disciple 2
Disciple 3
Disciple 4
Disciple 5
Townsperson 1
Townsperson 2
Narrator

Props: Flames made from construction paper and fastened to top of wooden dowels

Background scenery: A room in Jerusalem

(Scene opens with disciple puppets flopped over the edge of the stage as if they are sad and discouraged.)

Disciple 1 I don't know about you guys, but I am in no mood for a Pentecost party.

Disciple 2 Me neither. I feel awful.

Disciple 3 When Jesus died on the cross, it was horrible. It was the saddest day of my life. Here it is, seven weeks later, and every day I feel worse instead of better.

Disciple 4 Pentecost is supposed to be a day of thanksgiving. What do we have to be thankful for?

Disciple 5 But Jesus told us to stay in Jerusalem until God sends us power from on high.

Disciple 1 I don't want power. I just want Jesus to come back.

(Wind sounds on a tape cassette work well here. Wind sounds continue as disciples speak.)

Disciple 1 What was that?

Disciple 2 Wind.

Disciple 3 That's more than wind! *(Puppets get blown around.)*

Disciples 4 & 5 Whoa!

(Flames on dowels appear dancing behind disciples.)

Disciple 1   Holy cow! Look at that. Flames jumping all over the place.

Disciple 2   Hey, there's a flame over your head. Someone get a bucket!

Disciple 3   There's one over your head, too.

Disciple 4   I'm afraid to look.

Disciple 5   Yep, it's there all right. Talk about special effects!

Disciple 1   Don't move anyone!

(Everyone begins talking in different languages at the same time, repeating the same line over and over.)

Disciple 1   Christus der retter.

Disciple 2   O Patris caritas.

Disciple 3   Jesus, nino de Dios.

Disciple 4   Jezu niu moja.

Disciple 5   Christe, re divin.

(Peter and the townspeople enter. This scene may include extra characters if the cast is large. Puppets continue to speak in different languages.)

Townsperson 1   What is all this ruckus? We heard strange sounds from the street.

Townsperson 2   I can't understand what they are saying.

Townsperson 1   This is weird. I know all of these men are from Galilee, and yet everyone is speaking in a different language.

Townsperson 2   It is strange! Well, maybe they just drank too much wine.

Peter   My friends, these people are not drunk. I will tell you about a wonderful thing that has happened. Long ago, the prophet Joel said that one day God would pour out the Holy Spirit on the believers of the faith, and that fire and wind and strange events would happen. Jesus Christ walked among us and we are his witnesses. He was the promised Messiah.

Townsperson 1   That makes no sense at all.

Peter   Oh yes, for it is all part of God's wonderful plan to fill our hearts with love and with the desire to spread the good news of Jesus Christ to every corner of the world.

Disiciple 1   Peter, what shall we do?

Disciple 2   Yes, we are all confused.

Peter   We must all turn from sin and be baptized in the name of Jesus Christ. Then you will receive the gift of the Holy Spirit.

Townsperson 1   And just what is this Holy Spirit thing!

Peter   The Holy Spirit is that special feeling, deep down inside you, that is God working within you. God sent Jesus Christ to show us how to live and love and care for one another, and now God has given the gift of the Holy Spirit to those who believe in Jesus Christ. The Holy Spirit will help you live the life that Jesus asked you to live.

Townsperson 2   Is this gift just for these special people?

Peter   No, my friend, it is for all who believe: you and you and you. Come, let me tell you about it.

Narrator   Peter sat and talked with the disciples and the people who gathered around. When he had finished, Peter baptized all those who chose to receive the gift of the Holy Spirit. Would you believe that there were 3,000 people baptized? Well, there were, and those followers told others and soon the good news of the story of Jesus Christ began to spread far and wide. That is why Pentecost is called the birthday of the church. For on that strange Pentecost day, God gave the gift of the Holy Spirit so that Christians would share love and caring with people everywhere. Ever since that day, Christians in the church have done that.

On the Road to Damascus
(Adapted from Acts 9)

Characters: Narrator
              Saul
              Two companions
              Ananias
              Voice of Jesus

Props: Background picture of road
         Background picture of city
         Flashlight

Scene One: Along the road

Narrator   This is a story about Saul, a very religious Jew and also a pharisee. In addition, he was a citizen of Rome. Sounds impressive, doesn't it? But Saul was not a nice person. He knew all about this Jesus of Nazareth who had just been crucified and Saul made it his business to pester and punish the followers of Jesus.

Companion 1   If we hurry, we can be in Damascus before rush-hour traffic.

Saul   Let's step on it, then. There are Christians in hiding there, and I intend to fine *every one* of them.

Companion 2   You really want to get these followers of Jesus, don't you? Why do they bother you so much?

Saul   These crazy Christians are enemies of Rome and they are upsetting the Romans and the pharisees. They are causing disorder everywhere.

Companion 1   Are they fighting? I thought this Jesus fellow preached love and peace.

Saul   No, they don't fight. But Jesus told them to obey God's laws and not Roman laws. And he threw all the shopkeepers out of the temple. Hard working men trying to make a living. Just wrecked their stalls and threw them out.

Companion 2   Why did he do that?

Saul   Oh, something about his father's house being a house of prayer and not a den of thieves. Imagine that! Like he had special privileges.

Companion 1	Sounds like a real troublemaker to me.

Saul Yep. That is why we got rid of him. Crucified him. But those Christians just won't give up. Now they say this Jesus keeps appearing to them....Unbelievable! When you're dead, you're dead. Right?

(Companions laugh loudly. Then a bright light appears.)

Saul Whoa! What's that light? Where is it coming from? Hey, stop! Turn it off!

Companions What is that? It's awesome! Wow!

Saul Stop! Stop! I can't see! Help me! Help me! I'm blind.

Voice of Jesus Saul! Saul! Why do you persecute me?

Saul Who is that? Lord, is it you?

Voice of Jesus I am Jesus whom you are persecuting. Get up and go into the city. There, you will be told what to do.

Saul Oh help! Help! I can't see a thing. I am really scared.

Companion 1 Here, let me help you.

Companion 2 This *is* scarey. *(Puppets leave.)*

Scene two: In the city

Narrator Meanwhile, Jesus spoke to a man named Ananias, who lived in the city.

Voice of Jesus Ananias, go to Straight Street and at the house of Judas ask for a man named Saul. He will be expecting you.

Ananias Him? Are you sure? Jesus, this Saul is a very dangerous man. He came here to arrest all the Christians!

Voice of Jesus I am sure. You must go, for I have chosen this man to carry my message to the whole world.

Scene three: In the city

Narrator And so, Ananias went and found Saul and laid his hand upon him.

Ananias Brother Saul, I am sent by Jesus, who appeared to you, so that you might have your sight back and receive the Holy Spirit. *(Ananias touches Saul's head.)*

Ananias And now, I will baptize you in the name of Jesus of Nazareth.

Narrator Saul's life was completely changed in that one wonderful moment. Something like fish scales fell from his eyes and he was able to see again. Saul later changed his name to Paul. He went on to become the greatest missionary in the history of the Christian faith as he spread the good news of the story of Jesus Christ wherever he went.

Paul, Silas, and the Earthquake
(Based on the story in Acts 16)

Characters: Narrator
     Paul
     Silas
     City Leader 1
     City Leader 2
     Judge
     Jailer

Props: Sword

Background scenery: In front of city jail

Narrator The apostle Paul had many exciting adventures on his missionary journeys, and he often faced danger. Still, he risked his life over and over as he struggled to bring the good news of Jesus Christ to all the world. One such adventure happened when Paul and Silas traveled to the city of Philipi in Greece. The city leaders became upset when Paul and Silas did some preaching and healing. They dragged Paul and Silas to see the city judge.

(City leaders enter dragging Paul and Silas. Judge also enters.)

City Leader 1 These Jews are corrupting our city.

Judge What have they done?

City Leader 2 They are teaching people to do things against Roman law.

Judge Ah, fellows, you are visitors here. You can't act like that in our city. I will have to sentence you to jail and also to be beaten with wooden whips. Case dismissed. *(Judge leaves.)*

(City leaders pretend to beat Paul and Silas. Sound effects backstage will help make this more dramatic.)

City Leader 1 Take that you stupid Jews. This will teach you to stop spreading your rubbish Christian nonsense to our people.

City Leader 2 Yeh, you big dummies!

City Leader 1 Now, into prison you go.

City Leader 2 *(to jailer)* If you let these two dogs escape, you will pay with your life.

Jailer Don't worry. I'm taking no chances. I'm going to put them in the inner dungeon and, just to be sure, I'm going to put their legs in chains.

(Takes Paul and Silas below stage. Door slamming and clanking noises will add to this action.)

City Leader 1 Good riddance! *(Both city leaders leave.)*

Jailer *(enters)* Well, they are locked up all safe and secure. I think I'll just take a little snooze here.

(From below stage, Paul and Silas sing a hymn, such as Jesus Loves Me. *Then rumbling and shaking begin and get louder.)*

Jailer *(Falls all around)* Whoa! What's going on? Whoa!

(Noises and shaking continue until jailer finally falls over and all becomes still.)

Jailer What happened? I remember. It must have been an earthquake. I had better check on the prisoners. *(Looks down.)* Oh no! The doors are all open. *(Looks down again.)* The chains are laying there. Oh no! The prisoners have escaped. Oh no! I'm done for. Oh no! Where is my sword? I might as well kill myself and save someone else the trouble. Goodbye, world!

Paul *(from below)* Hey, up there! Don't do it!

Jailer What?

Silas We are down here.

Jailer *(Looks surprised. Goes below stage and brings Paul and Silas up.)* You could have escaped and you didn't. You are truly good and honest men. Oh, my friends, please forgive me.

Silas Of course, we do.

Jailer Sirs, what must I do to be saved?

Paul Come, let us talk.

Narrator All through the night, Paul and Silas talked with the jailer. Then they baptized him. He rejoiced because now he was a believer. The next morning the judge and the city leaders came by.

Judge   Let these men go!

Jailer   *(in disbelief)* What?

City Leader 1   Let them go because we don't want any public uprising over this. With the earthquake and all, people are beginning to wonder if this has anything to do with it.

Jailer   Great! Now you are both free to go.

Paul   Not on your life. We have been publicly beaten and jailed without a trial and we are Roman citizens. Now you want to sneak us out of here? No way!

Silas   Yes, you know your lives are in danger because you treated citizens of Rome in this way.

City Leader 1   Oh please, sirs. We will do anything only please just leave our city.

City Leader 2   We made a mistake. We are sorry.

Judge   We won't bother your Christian friends and we will allow you to meet with them again. Only please go from here and leave Philipi as soon as possible.

Paul   Well, O.K. We have sown the seeds of the faith here anyway. We can leave because we know the church here will continue to grow and grow.

Narrator   Then Paul and Silas forgave those who had punished them. They said farewell to their jailer friend and met with their Christian friends in Philipi one more time. Paul and Silas then continued on their way, spreading the good news of Jesus Christ wherever they traveled.

Philip and the Ethiopian
(Based on Acts 8)

Characters: Narrator
             Philip
             Angel
             Ethiopian

Props: Chariot (flat side only, but both sides should be finished.)
        Horse

Background scenery: Along a desert road

Narrator   Shortly after the death and resurrection of Jesus, many of the followers had to leave Jerusalem because they were in danger there. In a way this was good, because it helped the early church to grow. Wherever they went, the good news of Jesus Christ was spread. One of these followers, Philip, had been a disciple. For a while, he taught in Samaria. It was not safe for Christians to stay in any one place for very long, so Philip decided to travel south from Jerusalem toward Africa. One morning, a strange thing happened.

Philip   It looks like it will be a very warm day. I'm glad I got an early start.

Angel   *(Appears)* Philip?

Philip   What in the world? Who are you? How do you know my name?

Angel   You are Philip, a disciple of Jesus of Nazareth, and I am a messenger from God.

Philip   But I have been preaching and teaching about our Lord and I gathered many new believers.

Angel   Right. And you are doing a good job, Philip, but God has a special job for you.

Philip   A special job?

Angel   Yes. Be at the second fork in the southern desert road tomorrow at high noon.

Philip   Wow! I'll have to hurry. What should I do when I get there.

Angel   Just go and meet a chariot. That is all I can say. Goodbye for now. *(Angel leaves.)*

Narrator So, Philip took off running. *(Philip runs back and forth across the stage.)* It was almost twelve o'clock the next day when he came near to a chariot along the road and in it was a man reading some Scriptures. As it happened, the man in the chariot was a *very* important person in Ethiopia. He was in charge of all the queen's money and property.

(Ethiopian appears at side of stage in a chariot.)

Philip Now, there is a really big man. He must be nearly seven feet tall and he is very dark, so he certainly must be from a southern country. Look at all those fine silks and jewels. He has to be someone important. *(Moves closer.)* O.K., God, what do I do now?

Ethiopian *(reading to himself)* The servant of the God has not sinned. He is innocent. Like a lamb he is led to slaughter. He does not protest. *(Looks up at Philip.)* Oh, hello there. I was just reading from these ancient Jewish Scriptures, but I cannot understand their meaning. Tell me, is the prophet Isaiah speaking of himself or is the man who suffers someone else?

Philip I think I can help you. Let's go for a little ride.

(Philip and Ethiopian get in the chariot and pretend to ride back and forth across stage.)

Narrator As they rode together, Philip told the Ethiopian all about Jesus of Nazareth, and how he was the one that Isaiah and all the prophets had talked about. Philip told how Jesus had come from God into the world, how he had suffered and died to save us all, and how he arose again.

Ethiopian I am very touched by all you say and I believe what you tell is true. Jesus Christ is the Son of God. Look! There is some water along the road. Will you baptize me?

Philip I can see that you do believe. Come. *(They leave the chariot and the Ethiopian kneels as Philip baptizes him.)* I baptize you in the name of the Father, and of the Son, and of the Holy Spirit. Now, go on your way and serve the Lord all the days of your life.

Ethiopian Thank you, my friend, for showing me the way. I am so happy and I want to tell everyone the good news you have shared with me.

Narrator Then Philip went on his way preaching and teaching, and the Ethiopian went on his way rejoicing and telling others about Jesus Christ.

Paul and the Shipwreck
(Based on the story in the Acts of the Apostles)

Characters: Narrator   Props: Side of a ship
              Ship Captain   Sticks
              Paul   Snake (braided yarn or paper)
              Islanders

                          Background scenery: At sea
                                                On the beach

Narrator   In the early days of the church, the first Christians bravely faced many dangers as they preached the good news of Jesus of Nazareth. Rulers and leaders were afraid that these Christians would stir up the people with new ideas. That is why the governor of Jerusalem arrested Paul and put him in jail. Paul had continued to preach the gospel of Jesus Christ, and sometimes this meant speaking out against Rome. Finally, the governor decided to send Paul to Rome to be tried before Caesar. That way, he could get Paul out of Jerusalem before Paul caused more trouble. Paul and some other prisoners were loaded onto a sailing ship and they set sail for Rome.

Scene One : At sea

(Puppets are all behind the flat side of a ship. It begins to rock and winds begin to blow.)

First Mate   There is a storm brewing, that's for sure.

Captain   Lower the sail. Fasten the hatches. *(swinging around)* And who are you?

Paul   I am Paul, sir. I think we should stop over on the island of Crete.

Captain   Oh you do, do you?

Paul   Yes sir. It is late in the season to make such a trip as this. It will be dangerous for us to go on.

Captain   May I remind you that I am in charge here. You are merely a prisoner. On to Rome.

(Boat rocks, winds blow, and puppets bounce all around.)

Paul   Have courage, everyone. No one will die. Only the ship will be destroyed.

Captain   Now how do you know that?

Paul   Last night, an angel from God came to me and said, "Do not be afraid. I tell you that you will reach Rome and God will preserve all those with you."

(Winds blow stronger and howl. Ship rocks harder.)

Captain   Now hear this! Lower the lifeboat! Abandon ship!

Paul   Wait! Please wait! You will all die unless everyone stays on board.

First Mate   I'm staying. I think this Paul knows what he's talking about. I'm not moving from this ship.

Captain   O.K.! O.K.! Cut the lifeboat loose. Everyone, stay put!

(Boat keeps rocking. Winds keep howling.)

Paul   *(Wind stops and boat rocks very gently.)* It is morning. We are safe. Come, everyone. The storm has had you troubled. Please eat something. You will need your strength. Here, let me give you some bread *(pretending to pass food)*.

Captain   The sea is calmer *(looking hrough a telescope)*. Land! I see land! Let us try to sail closer.

(Boat rocks, then stops quickly. Puppets jerk.)

First Mate   Oh, no! We've hit bottom. The ship is going to break apart.

Captain   Tell everyone to jump overboard and swim to shore.

First Mate   We'd better kill all of the prisoners, for if they swim to shore, they will try to escape.

Captain   No time for that! Anyway, if the poor devils make it to shore, they will be too tired to run far. *(yells)* Abandon ship!

Scene Two: On the Beach

Narrator   Well, Paul and the other prisoners did make it safely to shore and so did the ship's crew. In fact, all 276 persons aboard that ship made it to the island safely. People on the island rushed down to the beach to help the victims of the shipwreck.

Islander   Welcome to the island of Malta.

Captain   Thank you, friends.

Islander   Here, let us make you warm and dry. Come, let us build a fire and then we will go and get you some food.

Paul   You are all very kind to help us. I can help gather wood for the fire. Let me get some of these sticks.

(Paul jumps back. A snake is attached to his hand. The puppet holds on to snake.)

Islander   Oh, no! A snake!

First Mate   It has bitten his hand and it's still holding tight.

Captain   He will surely die.

Islander   He must be a murderer. Even though he escaped drowning, he must pay for his sins. Justice will not allow him to live.

(Paul shakes the snake loose, drops it into the fire, and continues to gather sticks.)

Captain   Look! He shook the snake into the fire.

First Mate   And Paul is still alive!

Islander   That man must be a god.

Paul   Come, my friends, let us rest awhile and I will tell you some good news.

Narrator   For three months, Paul and the others stayed on the island. Paul preached to the people and healed those who were ill. When a ship arrived to take the travelers on to Rome, the people of the island loaded the ship with all sorts of things needed for the trip. They were grateful to Paul for all he had done for them. Paul showed love and compassion for others all through the storm, the shipwreck, and the months on the island. He showed Christians how to treat one another, just as Jesus had said we should do.
